Turning Your Scars into Stars

Chronic Abandonment and Rejection
that Life Experiences Brings

Edith Dolores Roman

authorHOUSE®

AuthorHouse™
1663 Liberty Drive
Bloomington, IN 47403
www.authorhouse.com
Phone: 1 (800) 839-8640

Published by AuthorHouse   09/02/2016

ISBN: 978-1-5049-8228-3 (sc)
ISBN: 978-1-5049-8229-0 (hc)
ISBN: 978-1-5049-8227-6 (e)

Library of Congress Control Number: 2016903381

"We cannot teach people anything; we can only help them discover it within themselves."

Galileo Galile

Contents

About The Author

Edith Dolores Roman was born at 4:01 AM on Thursday, February 3, 1949 at St. Anthony's Hospital in Denver, Colorado. Orphaned at the age of eleven, she became a ward of the court. Edith is now living in the Central Coast of California.

The following are some of Edith's accomplishments:

- Real Estate Board of Realtors Million Dollar Club member

- **Oakland Tribune** front page: "From Rags to Riches, Edith had nowhere to go but up." Page 2 – "It took gumption for Edith to make good; Successful real estate broker was on welfare five years ago."

- **The Central Coast Tribune** front page: "Helps Family from Welfare to Owning a Home, and assisted two other Spanish-speaking Latino families – one living in a trailer in a strawberry field and another also a labor field-worker family. A third family of five were living in a small apartment, and it took nine months for their dream to come true."

- **The Times Valley Today** front page: Realtor Plaque appeared on page 6 of Tom Hopkins – How to Master the Art of Listing Real Estate – Testimony."

- Has been a landlord for thirty-two years for tenants needing a second chance in Hayward, Newark and Pismo Beach, California.

- Speaker at Professional National Speakers Association and won the Best Table Topic Award.

- Attended Avila Modeling School and left with three honorable mentions.

- Certificate of Achievement from Chabot College, speaking to single mothers coming off of welfare in Hayward, California.

- Award from the Central Coast Business Center for "Most Courageous Woman" for her extraordinary courage and inspiration.

- After losing her wallet, which contained $900 in cash, Edith placed an ad in a local newspaper and an honest woman who found the wallet responded to the plea and returned the wallet with all the cash inside. Edith gave her a handsome reward.

- Schools Attended in California: Portola Junior High in San Francisco, graduated 6/11/64; Woodrow Wilson High in San Francisco, graduated 6/14/67. Majored in Home Economics and Business.

- Employment History in Calfornia: Worked part-time in a privately-owned lingerie store and as a clerk at Macy's Warehouse, both located in San Francisco. Operated machinery-making envelopes from 1967-1969. Was a Quality Control person, checking each item before shipping, from 1969-1970; Cardboard Factory from 1970-1971 in Burlingame.

- In 1973 became a Real Estate Agent.

- In 1973 became a Real Estate Broker and Notary.

- Specializes in helping first-time buyers qualify and turn seemingly impossible situations into miracles. Example: qualified a 50-year old gentleman who had always rented and had never used his GI Bill; helped those on welfare bankruptcies and poor credit clean up their credit.

- Humorous Accomplishment: Purchased a Rolls Royce for $8 instead of $8,000. Edith didn't realize she had written the check incorrectly; neither did the dealership until it was cashed! She, of course, rectified her mistake

- First time author – "Turning Your Storms Into Rainbows," a book that was published worldwide.

- Currently offers consulting services in Real Estate, Property Management, Becoming an Author, and Gourmet Cooking. Email her at roman_realty@yahoo.com

Introduction

I was so happy when I found out that Edith was writing a book to address overcoming emotional scars from the past and how to face challenges in life. I am always saddened when I hear about people who avoid turning to Jesus because the enemy has lied to them and tried to convince them that they are not worthy of redemption. The enemy tries to break people down with abuse and pain. He tries to make them think that there is something wrong with them, that they are too dirty or broken to be the type of shiny, happy, perfect people that they think go to church. They believe that God is disappointed or disgusted with them, and that they have no chance to become one of His beloved sons or daughters. The devil is a liar indeed, and this book proves that *no one* is too far from God's healing hand. This book also addresses the fact that when a person finally does find the courage to dedicate their lives to Jesus, their life is not going to be a carefree walk in the park. In fact, they may suddenly be bombarded with trials, persecution, and challenges that they didn't face when they were not Christian because now the enemy is angry that he has lost a soul, and turns to attack them with vengeance. This book explains the different types of situations that we face in life. Edith has chosen to distinguish them as different types of "lights" like the red, yellow, and green traffic lights used to give instruction to drivers. In her writings, she explains the different types of situations life may throw at us and how to face them. We should not react naively as young children, nor should we be reactive or worldly in our response. We should instead take the time to evaluate the situation and try to understand what lesson or test God is putting before us. We should pray and submit ourselves to His will and know the simple teachings that we should live by as Christians. For example, we must be careful of being prideful because pride comes before a fall; we should forgive others, because the measure of forgiveness we use towards others is the measure of forgiveness that will be used toward us; we should in all situations, even in ones where we are being wronged by an enemy, remember that Jesus always wants us to act in love toward our fellow man. God also has blessings for us in stow that we should be brave enough to take hold of. We should pray for his blessings because His Word says that we do not have because we do not ask. We must believe and know that God's plans for us are to prosper us and not to harm us, to give us a hope and a future. I encourage you to read this book and share it with others. Let it motivate you to build your foundation in the Lord each and every day. We never know when our day of testing will come, so I pray that this book and its teachings will strengthen you against the attacks of the enemy. "Therefore, put on the full armor of God, so that when the day of evil comes, you may be able to stand your ground, and after you have done everything, to stand." Ephesians 6:13

Ogochukwu Agbo

Edith's Story

My father Henry Jack Miller died when I was three years old. That is the first hit which life threw at me that I can remember. He was a very excellent entrepreneur who owned a large hardware store for many years. He was well-known in Denver, Colorado and respected in the community for being a man that often helped people in need. I was his baby girl out of four children and the apple of his eye. He would always tell me I looked like Shirley Temple with green eyes. He used to take me to buy an ice cream cone and sit me up on the parlor counter. "What flavor would you like? Vanilla? Strawberry? Chocolate?" he would ask me, and for each suggestion I would shrug my shoulders because I didn't know. So then he would look at the waitress with his beautiful blue eyes and tell her "Just give her all three flavors!" Although my father was a beautiful soul, he struggled with alcoholism and died from cirrhosis of the liver when I was three years old, leaving me heartbroken.

Another huge scar on my life was when my mother Estelle Ruth Trujillo-Miller died. She was the youngest beautician in the state of Colorado and owned her own beauty salon where she was fortunate to work for many movie stars. She was very much a perfectionist, and so when she got me ready for pictures and special events she would always make sure that every curl was in place and that I was dressed cutely in lace socks, white patent-leather shoes, and cashmere coats. She was very proud of me as I was her first child, born to her when she was 28. As talented as my mother was, she struggled with mental disorders and alcoholism, so at the age of 11 I had to help take care of her and my younger sister, who had a broken neck from a car accident. My mother also eventually died from cirrhosis of the liver when she was 39 years old, and I was left as an orphan. No relatives or family friends would take me in, so I was forced to become a ward of the court at age 11. Soon afterwards, I was living alone in a youth guidance center and I got a serious infection in my left leg. The doctors told me that I would have to have my leg amputated and I was terrified. I stayed up all night the day before the scheduled operation praying to God to have mercy on me and heal my leg, and in a miracle, the growth burst and my leg was saved! I went on to live in a foster home for five years in San Francisco, CA. I obeyed my parents and teachers, did what I was told, and never got into trouble. I enjoyed getting involved with extracurricular activities, and when I went to Woodrow Wilson high school I liked doing things where I got to work with money. I was elected to be the treasurer for my homeroom and also helped to lead fundraisers like selling chocolate bars and dance tickets. In June 1967 I graduated from high school and a couple months later on August 5, 1967 I married a man named Francisco Roman. Nine months later had my first son on September 1, 1968 and named him Francisco after his father. Two and a half years later I bought a home in Daly City and gave birth to my daughter Cassandra Denise on February 26, 1971. Within the space of five years I had gotten married, bought a home, and had two children, and I had no idea what I was doing! I find it shocking that you need more training to get a driver's license than have a child or get married!

Unfortunately, my marriage ended after five years. After the divorce I was a single mother trying to support my two children without any outside help, so I was forced to go on welfare. I went into real estate to become a real estate agent and became a workaholic. I achieved a great deal of success in the real estate business and started using my commission checks to buy up extra rentals. I even was able to purchase a Rolls Royce! I remarried and continued to work long hard hours because I did not want to be on welfare. I eventually succeeded in paying back all the welfare money to the state, and even was published in a newspaper article for doing so! After the second marriage ended a few years later, I continued to work as a real estate agent and became a real estate broker. I received an honor for being one of the youngest brokers in the state of California to become part of the 'Million Dollar Club' by selling a million dollars worth of real estate and was featured on the front page of the Oakland Tribune.

In my later years, I realized that no amount of money was going to give me complete fulfillment. I changed gears from being a tireless workaholic to being a spirit-led Christian who was focused on doing the will of my savior, Jesus Christ. In my senior years I dedicated my life to showing others the love of God through fellowshipping with my church and mentoring those going through difficulty in their lives. Through deep prayer, I reached out to God to find my true purpose in life, and He put the desire to write a book on my heart. I was very intimidated and resistant to try to write a book because I didn't believe I was capable. I even prayed for God to release me from the assignment which I knew he had put before me. However, God's power was stronger than my lack of confidence, so after 17 and half years, I was elated to finally finish publishing my first book, "Turning Your Storms Into Rainbows," which became a worldwide-distributed book which changed and saved many lives. One sign of God's amazing grace is that on the very day that the book was published, I looked out my window and saw a magnificent rainbow reaching from the mountain to the ocean. Right then and there, I fell on my knees with immense gratitude as I realized that God loved me and believed in me more than even I did for myself. I knew that day that

His words in Jeremiah 29:11 were true; "'For I know the plans I have for you,' declares the Lord, 'plans to prosper you and not to harm you, plans to give you hope and a future'" (NIV).

The scars on my heart run deep. When my father died, I lost the gift of having a father to give me wisdom, teach me how to protect myself, and show me what a loving man is like. When my mother died I missed the security and safety of having a mother lead me through childhood and adolescence to womanhood. I was never able to have my parents present for special events like my graduation, buying my first home, and giving birth to my children. However, this book is about how God can turn scars, the deep and painful parts of our past, into stars, the joyful and constructive highlights of our future. The star that came from the scar of losing my parents is that my experiences led me to write about my life. Now I have become a worldwide-published author and have written this book which you now hold. The star which comes from the scar of painful loneliness I endured is that I came to know the infinite love of God. This second book, "Turning Your Scars Into Stars," has been an effort for more than ten years. What I have learned for myself, and what I want you to know now, is that no matter how long it takes to turn a scar into a star, it's worth it! Even if you are bloody, beaten, and bruised on the ground, reach for God's hand and get back up. The star is worth it. Keep going!

RED LIGHT

RED LIGHT

I decided that to represent the topic of this book, I would use an example of something in life that we are all familiar with: a traffic light. A traffic light has red, yellow and green lights. Red represents when tragedy strikes our lives - we stop in our tracks. Yellow is when we pause. Green is when we step on the gas and continue onto our destination.

A favorite scripture of mine is **Romans 8:31: "If God is for us, who can be against us?" (NIV).** This is one of my favorite verses because it helps me to remember that God is always with me and is always on my side. It helps me to persevere through the difficult, stressful, '911' emergency times in my life.

When we receive bad news such as health problems, financial challenges, the death of a loved one, or something very intense that we did not expect, it can be completely devastating. These are "red lights." The automatic response is to feel anxiety, the exact opposite response of the one our Lord wants us to have.

Red light issues bring fear and anxiety. One scripture that has comforted me throughout my life when these type of issues arise says that during times trouble, God wants us to remember His faithfulness:

Isaiah 41:10, "So do not fear, for I am with you; do not be dismayed, for I am your God. I will strengthen you and help you; I will uphold you with my righteous right hand" (NIV).

I am right handed, and the majority of people in the world are right handed. Our dominant hand is our stronger hand. Also, the right hand has traditionally been the "blessed" hand – that is why we when we meet people we use our right hand to shake hands. So, in this verse our dear Lord explains that He will use His right hand to bless us, and He does not want us to be dismayed. He will strengthen us, He will help us and He will uphold us throughout these tragic times.

Another verse I find helpful and often say to myself out loud is **Philippians 4: 6-7: "Do not be anxious about anything, but in every situation, by prayer and petition, with thanksgiving, present your requests to God. And the peace of God, which transcends all understanding, will guard your hearts and your minds in Christ Jesus" (NIV)**

This verse is my rock. However, for me, to not be anxious about anything is difficult. Every single day I have to work on releasing all my fears and concerns to God. He tells us 'Do not be anxious about anything.' That means everything from A to Z! So I go to Him for forgiveness, unconditional love, without fearing judgment, and I can release those things that I am anxious about to Him. I receive such a tremendous sense of relief when I unload it all on His shoulders! I am under construction. We are ALL under construction. When we offer forgiveness, unconditional love, and non-judgment to others, we are being like Jesus. Try to hold these thoughts in the center of your heart and mind and you will be full of grace, love, forgiveness and hope. You will find that there is not as much anxiety and fear in your daily life, and will feel much more comforted.

Deuteronomy 31:6 advises us **"Be strong and courageous. Do not be afraid or terrified because of them, for the Lord your God goes with you; he will never leave you nor forsake you" (NIV).**

I was an orphan, and became a ward of the court at a young age. My father died when I was three years young and my mother died when I was 11 years.

As a ward of the court I lived as a foster child for five very intense years. I did the best I could in school. I tried to be obedient. I didn't do drugs or alcohol or disobey my caretakers. However, every night I cried myself to sleep not knowing what would happen next. Yet, somehow God provided everything I needed. Not always what I wanted, but what I needed. I cling to the following verses, and I hope they help you too.

John 14:18 "I will not leave you as orphans; I will come to you" (NIV).

Isaiah 1:17 "Learn to do right; seek justice. Defend the oppressed. Take up the cause of the fatherless; plead the case of the widow" (NIV).

Psalm 27:10 "Though my father and mother have forsaken me, the Lord will receive me" (NIV).

Psalm 68:5 "A father to the fatherless, a defender of widows, is God in his holy dwelling" (NIV).

Psalm 34:18: "the Lord is close to the brokenhearted and saves those who are crushed in spirit" (NIV).

Psalm 147:3: "He heals the brokenhearted and binds up their wounds" (NIV).

Psalm 27:14: "Wait for the Lord; be strong and take heart and wait for the Lord" (NIV).

Psalm 34:6: "This poor man called, and the Lord heard him; he saved him out of all his troubles" (NIV).

John 16:33: "I have told you these things, so that in me you may have peace. In this world you will have trouble. But take heart! I have overcome the world" (NIV).

I quickly learned after becoming an orphan, a ward of the court, and then a foster child that I should not cause any conflict. I had to keep my desires, feelings and problems to myself. My past taught me not to talk, trust, or feel, and that I needed to please others to survive. It is grieving to think about how often many of us have had to suppress our basic desires to be heard, seen, and valued, and consequently have intense abandonment hurts that leave scars for decades or even a lifetime. As I continue to go through life I am continually trying to understand how and why I evolved the intense need to please others.

These issues of uncertainty, abandonment, and disappointment arise years later time and time again. For example, if I am told something about plans with a friend, and then later in the midst of planning something changes the plan, my whole world turns upside down. It is like we were driving along on a relaxing journey and suddenly there is a huge orange detour sign. My immediate inner thought is to panic. 'Oh no! A detour! How will I deal with this?' I am not comfortable with detours. When the unknown takes place in our life, there is something very awkward and unnerving about it for most of us. It is not a comfortable or familiar place, and most of the time detours take us places that we have never been. The best we can do is to try to be prepared, relax, and take a deep breath. Then we must reassess the situation and our part in the detour. Life has lots of changes for us. I have to admit that I do not want to adjust to changes, but I have to. Be flexible and adjust to changes that others bring if it is agreeable and takes you to the same end. If we don't adjust, the red light just remains red longer.

There have been difficult situations with people I have known for decades. Things have happened in my life as well as in theirs. At times we haven't kept in regular communication and our friendship seems to crumble away. I have suffered lots of pain and had lots of questions when these things happened and bring up my abandonment issues. When something is not resolved or is resolved unfavorably, it can cause another scar, a red light. We are scarred internally on our hearts... ouch!

If our heart is not closed to evil things such as fear, anxiety, injustice, and hating our enemy, we are imbalanced. The imbalance is like a cancer that manifests into our heart, spirit, and soul. Hate, anger, rage, and envy all create a discord in all areas of our life that prevents us from prospering. This causes another red light. I have never met a person who does not have an adversary. I continually have to tell myself to love and pray for my enemy. It is difficult for us to truly grasp that concept. If my enemy knocks on my door asking for help, according to God's word I should provide it to them. As the Bible says in **Proverbs 3:27, "Do not withhold good from those to whom it is due, when it is in your power to act" (NIV).**

A handful of verses that have helped me to rise above my feelings or hurts are below:

Ephesians 4:32 "Be kind and compassionate to one another, forgiving each other, just as in Christ God forgave you" (NIV).

Luke 17:3-4 "So watch yourselves. If your brother or sister sins against you, rebuke them; and if they

repent, forgive them. Even if they sin against you seven times a day and seven times come back to you saying 'I repent,' you must forgive them" (NIV).

Luke 6:37 "Do not judge, and you will not be judged. Do not condemn, and you will not be condemned. Forgive, and you will be forgiven."

Colossians 3:13 "Bear with each other and forgive one another if any of you has a grievance against someone. Forgive as the Lord forgave you" (NIV).

Luke 6:27-28 "But to you who are listening I say: Love your enemies, do good to those who hate you, bless those who curse you, pray for those who mistreat you" (NIV). Now isn't that a difficult thing to do!? I know that we all struggle with this request of Jesus. However, I assure you, loving your enemy causes something to happen to that person. When we give them what they need, when we give them unconditional love and forgiveness, they soften. God will allow the enemy to test you, so that you achieve a higher a level of *agape* love, the type of love that God has for us. When we come away from the battle without fighting back we are reflecting Jesus' manner. These types of situations lead us to find perfect peace in God's care and understanding. God's word says in **Philippians 4:7 "The peace of God, which transcends all understanding, will guard your hearts and your minds in Christ Jesus" (NIV).** When we come away from the battle without fighting back, it takes away the forum for the battle to continue. Nothing good happens when we attack each another; something good DOES happen when we love our enemies. I once heard a sermon that said that Judas was the most important disciple because without him and his betrayal of Jesus, the rest of humanity would not have the opportunity to inherit eternal life.

In the book of John in chapter 13, Jesus washes the feet of his disciples. This is a powerful example of how we should love our enemies, because even though Jesus knew Judas was planning to betray him, Jesus still washed Judas' feet also.

Proverbs 3:5 "Trust in the Lord with all your heart and do not lean on your own understanding" (NIV). Each and every time I have leaned on my own understanding, it has become a disaster. When I lean on the Lord I have peace, contentment, and tranquility, and I have no fear and anxiety because I have released them. Release things causing you angst in your home and in your relationships. Sometimes we even have to release people that are stifling our spiritual growth. We must remove ourselves from situations that cannot help us to grow.

Proverbs 25:21-22 "If your enemy is hungry, give him food to eat; if he is thirsty give him water to drink. In doing this, you will heap burning coals on his head, and the Lord will reward you" (NIV). Now here, saying that we will heap coals on our enemy's head is not meant to promote vindictive actions. It means that the Lord wants us to be the better person to our enemy, and in that way affect their conscience. When the Word says that our kind actions toward the enemy 'heap coals on his head,' it means that when we respond kindly and provide love and forgiveness, then our enemy may begin to feel repentant about way they have treated us. It is unfortunate that every single one of us will have enemies! The action of loving, forgiving, and serving our enemies does not come naturally and is very difficult. However, it is possible with the grace and love that only God can provide to us. If we look at most situations in our past, we see that our enemies helped us to grow closer to God because we turned to God in our times of desperation and persecution. If I look throughout my life, in different situations I have learned a great deal through my challenges with my adversaries. I hate to admit that at times, I have acted in a similar fashion as some of my enemies. However, I have learned to be humble, to release my will, and give it all to the Lord more and more.

Proverbs 15:18 "A hot-tempered person stirs up conflict, but the one who is patient calms a quarrel" (NIV). Another great verse for husband and wives is **Colossians 3:19 "Husbands, love your wives and do not be harsh with them" (NIV).**

I mentor five women and three couples and I lead the women to read and apply Proverbs 31 to their lives, which speaks about "The Wife of Noble Character." It is not easy for a wife to be humble and quiet when she disagrees with her husband. However, when a woman is very close to God she can do this. I am not saying that a woman should be a doormat – she should be highly loved and respected. It enhances a marriage when the husband adores his wife and treats her with the utmost respect.

I have a dear friend who is married to a good man. She shared with me that sometimes her husband drinks too much and his personality changes for the worst. He withdraws, neglects her, and shuts down emotionally. When he does this, she takes the credit card and goes to a nice hotel to stay for the night. The problem with her behavior is that her husband was abandoned as a child by his parents at age eleven. Therefore, when she leaves for the hotel, the scar of abandonment is ripped open again. I explained to her from my own experience how painful that must be for him. She was thankful for me opening her eyes to the hurts that were being inflicted when she left. Only then was she finally able to see that she was creating feelings of insecurity and abandonment in him that threatened the relationship. She never did it again, and today their marriage is on solid ground.

We should examine our actions under a microscope. We should ask ourselves, 'Is this going to be helpful long-term, or just a quick fix? Will what I choose to do right now to create a positive outcome?' The main thing we want to achieve, like when we are weeding a yard, is to pull the root out of the weed so it doesn't take root again. We need to eliminate the strongholds that create negativity in our lives.

Does forgiveness come naturally? I have done interviews with many people and asked them this question. Overwhelmingly, the answer they give is 'absolutely not!' It takes a great deal of the Holy Spirit, prayer, and denying ourselves in order to give the forgiveness needed to those who have offended or hurt us. I was recently called into the church for a meeting with the Pastor. A few parishioners had accused me unjustly of offending them. It wasn't something serious, but I don't normally remain silent when I am being slandered. I listened to the situation and didn't say a word. I just listened. As I sat there, I had a vision of Jesus hanging on the cross, walking the path he took on his journey to the mountaintop carrying the burden of our sin on the cross. He was mocked, beaten, spit on, humiliated, stabbed, given sour vinegar, nailed on his hands and feet, and forced to wear a crown of thorns. Although he never defended himself, he was, and still is, innocent and free of sin. I thought to myelf that if Jesus was innocent and endured all of that for me, then I can be silent and endure this for him. But it was difficult! I live in a carnal body, and on a daily basis I have to cleanse, repent, and pray. I visualize my whole entire body bowing down at Jesus' feet. Every day I come to ask forgiveness, and the wonderful thing is that God always supplies us with forgiveness grace and mercy. I am restored anew in His mercy. My hope is renewed.

Another big red light area is trauma of the past, and we must learn self-forgiveness to move past it. When I finally understood the concept of self-forgiveness, it changed my life. We all have replayed negative scenarios, going over them again and again in our minds, continually recalling situations of abuse, both verbal and physical. This rumination is insanity and it doesn't help us at all. It is re-traumatizing. We must learn to forgive ourselves. One day when I was stewing in negative thoughts about my past, I thought to myself, 'Why am I doing this to myself? That situation is over, it is dead and gone. No one else is thinking about it anymore, I have to let it go!' I was abusing myself by repeating it in my mind. I found that I had to completely release it, cleanse my mind of it, and give it over to God.

In my interviews with other people this same malady kept appearing. They found it difficult to forgive themselves and continued to abuse themselves up mentally by reliving traumatic scenarios in their heads. This self-torment is like a virus that blocks any good thing such as love, joy, peace, and tranquility from entering our lives. This self-inflicted virus blocks communication, connection, and intimacy. When you begin to ruminate on something that is causing you anguish, recognize the thought and immediately begin talking with

God about it. He will conform our thoughts to what is good and pure. Below is scripture that has been nourishing soul food for me:

John 5:30 "By myself I can do nothing; I judge only as I hear, and my judgment is just, for I seek not to please myself but him who sent me" (NIV).

2 Timothy 1:7 "For the Spirit God gave us does not make us timid, but gives us power, love and self-discipline" (NIV).

Red lights of fear, physical and verbal abuse, addictions, or any negative thing all cause separation. They separate us from others and from our loving God who created us to have full, whole, loving relationships with others and, most importantly, with Him. Separation opens the door to allow the enemy to attack your soul. If you notice someone under the influence of a chemical substance, their spirit is completely different from what it is like when they are connected to God. When they are connected to God, they can be loving and kind. They can share with you whatever you may need. They are able to pray for you and with you. On the other hand, when they under the influence of a chemical substance, they can be angry, abandoning, volatile, and unable to be reasoned with. The altered state they are in breaks down all communication, peace, and reasoning, causing frustration on both parts. This is why it is so vital to be very careful of what we touch, see, hear, and think, because what we allow into our heart, spirit, and soul ends up being transferred to the people we encounter and the situations in which we interact. I hope the following verse helps you as it does me.

Luke 6:45 (NIV) "A good man brings good things out of the good stored up in his heart, and an evil man brings evil things out of the evil stored up in his heart. For the mouth speaks what the heart is full of" (NIV).

Gossip and slander are two more red lights. I have noticed that if I am explaining a situation to another person or people, I tend to tell it in a way that benefits me and does not benefit the person I had a disagreement with. This is a form of slander, although it may seem a natural effect of human nature. When someone is telling me of a situation and the other party who is not present is being presented negatively, I have to halt the gossip because the other person is not there, and it is not right to speak badly of people behind their backs. A scripture verse that has greatly helped me to value this aspect of my integrity is **Proverbs 11:13 "A gossip betrays a confidence, but a trustworthy person keeps a secret" (NIV)**

This verse has also aided me greatly in my mentoring of others. We read God's Word and can be assured that there will be no gossiping or slandering of others during our mentoring time.

How can one avoid gossip? One key strategy is to not associate with gossipers! Others will assume that you are a gossiper also. When in a situation where you are witnessing gossip or slander, obey your conscience and do not participate. Change the subject, or interrupt and say, "I really don't need all the details. God knows the truth, and the best thing we can do is to pray for them." If you are not part of the problem or solution, then stay out of it! If you have fallen into the bad habit of gossiping, pray and ask God to change your heart. I admit that it is tempting at times to gossip, but when we talk about anything negative it then it only gains power. Gossip and slander create unhealthy relationships, and they endanger your own reputation. Stop and pause before you speak. Last but not least, when you have been the victim of gossip or slander, be brave enough to deal with the parties that are spreading the rumor. Communication is necessary to prevent the spreading of misinformation.

James 3:2 "We all stumble in many ways. Anyone who is never at fault in what they say is perfect, able to keep their whole body in check" (NIV).

1 Peter 2:1 "Therefore, rid yourselves of all malice and all deceit, hypocrisy, envy, and slander of every kind" (NIV).

I live near the beach. I find it very refreshing to go to the beach to pray and sort through the things that are happening in my life with God. It is important that you find your sanctuary also. You can go anywhere that gives you comfort and solitude and lets you feel God surrounding you. I like to go places where I can be relaxed by elements of nature. Go to your special place and do things to help you find peace, for example listening to a faith-based radio channel or your favorite soothing music. Read the Bible, pray, and look for the good in whatever situation you are going through. We need to look for the good in people and relationships. I have noticed that when I review a negative situation, I am able put what I am feeling into words rather than just raw emotions. When God moves me to go in love to the person whom I feel wronged me to discuss the situation, the issue always resolves favorably. It is a lot of hard work to communicate and have relationships. It is not easy and there is only one all-encompassing manual: the Bible! It is a lot of work to make peace with ourselves and with other people. However, no matter how difficult they are, relationships and the hard work that goes along with them are absolutely worth the effort. We were meant to be in relationship, it is how God made us – he created Eve because it was not good that Adam should be alone. The best soul food is to keep ourselves at the feet of Jesus with prayer, with praises, with the power of His love and the good words of wisdom found in the Bible.

A comforting verse is **Zephaniah 3:17 "The Lord your God is with you, the Mighty Warrior who saves. He will take great delight in you; in his love he will no longer rebuke you, but will rejoice over you with singing" (NIV).**

There is nothing that comes close or supersedes the joy of when we are in the power, presence, and the provision of our Lord. The red lights we have talked about will pull us away from God and his holy plan.

Jeremiah 29:11 "'For I know the plans I have for you,' declares the Lord, 'plans to prosper you and not to harm you, plans to give you hope and a future'" (NIV).

I just finished a 3-month course on oppression and depression, which is another red light topic. I believe that all of us have a bout of depression at some point in our lives, to some degree. I call these difficult times in life '911s'. When a 911 happens in our lives we shut down. It can be anything that overloads us. We can be immobilized by oppression or depression. For some, this time is more debilitating than the same situation may be for others. In my case, no one seems to believe I am depressed, sobbing and crying in private, because in public

I am driven to accomplish and I force myself to persevere through my problems, masking what I am going through. The world looks at us and judges us based on our accomplishments. When you help others, the perception others have of you is that you must be doing great for yourself. This is simply not true; it is a way to cover up your own suffering and stay in the pain of hurt, discouragement and abandonment. We need to confront the oppression and depression. It won't just go away just because we hope that it will. We need to seek help, read God's handbook on life – the Bible - and take good care of ourselves.

For 33 years I have mentored a young lady in Denver that I will call "Grace." We are very close and I had the privilege of baptizing Grace seven years ago. Well unfortunately, time slipped away and for a while we lost touch. We reconnected when she called me to share her wonderful news of having reconnected with a young gentleman,

"Jay," she had dated from her high school years. It was a miracle and a rainbow moment for me. She shared with me how I had deeply impacted her life and how now she was impacting others. She had baptized Jay and he had asked her to marry him. Her call was to invite me to walk her down the aisle as her spiritual mother, because of the impact I had made in her life. I am honored to do so and look forward to my trip back to Denver for the momentous occasion. What a blessing to see God's hand at work! The point here is that God is working even when we don't know it. Like the underground of a beautiful rose or plant, we cannot see the roots that are growing and penetrating through the deep soil underground. We don't feel or see it happening. Over the phone I chatted a bit with Jay, a wonderful man. He told me he had been in the pit of despair for three years. He also said the following to me which I really appreciated: "When we are in the pit, God takes us to the palace!" The wonderful payoff of this journey is that in a few months they will be married. Who back then would have known that in 33 years they would be married?! They weren't ready 33 years ago coming out of high school. They had to go through the trials and tribulations for decades that made them who they are today. The Lord says that we should count all our trials as joy!

Romans 12:12 "Be joyful in hope, patient in affliction, faithful in prayer" (NIV).

Through prayer and trust in God, in one second the whole situation can and will change. Just like that, a red light can change to green. We must trust God. We don't know what the future will bring, but we know who holds it.

James 1:2 "Consider it pure joy, my brothers and sisters, whenever you face trials of many kinds" (NIV). Even I have to admit that I haven't quite accomplished that level of maturity. It is a challenge when the pain, the hurt, and the trials are long and heavy. For example, the very act of writing this book, "Turning Your Scars Into Stars," has taken over ten years. Writing this book has been a project for a decade! My first book, "Turning Your Storms Into Rainbows," took 17 and a half years to write. It produced miracles, including changing some lives and saving others. These books are labors of love. They were birthed into reality many years after God planted a seed into me of the desire to become an author. I originally prayed for Him to find someone else to write these books, because I certainly did not feel qualified to become an author. However, the desire surprisingly intensified and became stronger than ever. The act of finally publishing these books was similar to a woman giving birth after months of pregnancy and a painful labor. I was tested financially, mentally, emotionally, and spiritually. God let His purpose for me grow in me, and eventually come forth to fruition. These books are for everyday reading, not for the shelf.

Deuteronomy 7:19 refers to when God reminds the Israelites of how He saved them from slavery in Egypt; "**You saw with your own eyes the great trials, the signs and wonders, the mighty hand and outstretched arm, with which the Lord your God brought you out. The Lord your God will do the same to all the peoples you now fear**" (NIV). This is the amazing grace of God that we should really try to grasp. He is always with us. I have interviewed people that have triumphed through challenges that I cannot even imagine. More often than not, they attribute their survival or recovery to God's intervention. I have a stepson who is world renowned for playing ice-hockey. He went to Russia and won three medals - gold, silver and bronze. One of his legs was blown off by a bomb in the Iraq War. However, he lives a full and victorious life! People with a challenge need to overcome that challenge, and many turn to God where they reap an intimacy like no other.

Every year, monarch butterflies migrate to the same field of trees by the ocean only a couple of miles away from where I live. One day when I was watching them I realized that when God is preserving us during all our red light situations, He is taking us through a transformation like one that a butterfly goes through. We are changed like a caterpillar that crawls into a cocoon but comes out as an amazing, beautiful butterfly that no longer crawls but flies. Perhaps you have heard the saying, 'the faith of a mustard seed will move mountains.' We have to have faith to weather the trials and faith to know God will get us through the storms to the other side. When the apostles asked Jesus for more faith, Jesus replied in **Luke 17:6 "If you have faith as small as a mustard seed, you can say to this mulberry tree, 'Be uprooted and planted in the sea,' and it will obey you" (NIV).** Jesus also said in **John 11:40: "'Did I not tell you that if you believe, you will see the glory of God?'" (NIV).** That is really incredible!!

Grief is another devastating red light. Part of the problem with it is that we never know how long it will take to feel normal again. I recently asked a lovely woman out to lunch to get to know her better. Her words and actions had drawn me to her spiritually. I learned during lunch that one of her sons had died and she did not know where the other son was. As I got to know her she spoke of many red lights, but she declared that she knew that the red lights would eventually change for the better. She asked me for prayer. To those who look at her there is no outward evidence of her grief - she is motivated, she always smiles, and she is an amazing positive woman. We need to follow her example and choose to focus on the good around us. In the midst of our troubles we must remember that we are still breathing; we still have a heartbeat, and this too shall pass.

I love that one of my favorite verses matches my last name: **Romans 12:12 says "Be joyful in hope, patient in affliction, faithful in prayer" (NIV).** What good father would not reach out and help their child? God longs to help us when we reach out to him. He waits for us to reach out to him and rejoices when we do. What I have learned from the trials and pains I have lived through is that sometimes life hurts. At times life is sad, it is discouraging, and can seem like a long, long journey, but God sees us through the storm. One thing I know for sure is that if we stay firm with the king, the master, the rock who made us in His image, that red light will change to green.

Psalm 77:11 "I will remember the deeds of the Lord; yes I will remember your miracles of long ago" (NIV). I recall the storms God has brought me through. He has so much mercy, grace and compassion at all times. Continue to kneel and pray because when we least expect it, we will be able to stand up victorious again. Remember, if we don't stand for something, we will fall for anything. Choose to stand for Christ. Stay fervent in prayer and praise Him for all things. Read his life instruction manual the Bible, and be refreshed. Other people are watching us, and if we are a good example of a faithful Christian, whatever we are going through can be of assistance to help them when they undergo their own challenges.

Each person that draws us to them is a treasure. They can give to us in areas in which we may be lacking, and we can also give to them. I attended a seminar and learned there are four different characters in a relationship. There is teacher, student, parent, and child. All four of these characters play a role in a friendship. A problem arises when the characters are out of balance, for example when both people act like teachers and control and manipulation become an issue. My favorite character is the child. I love to play and be unburdened with the daily grind of responsibilities like work, finances, and household maintenance. I love how a child has the freedom to be their true self, to laugh, have fun, and play. God designed us to be like little children!

He tells us that 'we should have faith as a little child.' In **Matthew 19:14** it is written **"Let the little children come to me and do not hinder them, for the kingdom of heaven belongs to such as these"** **(NIV). Matthew 18:3**, a beautiful verse, says **"Truly I tell you, unless you change and become like little children, you will never enter the kingdom of heaven" (NIV).**

Another serious red flag issue is mental illness. It seems that people can respect seeing someone with an impaired limb, a disease, or any type of physical disorder. However, many do not have mercy or understanding for those whom are challenged with mental health illnesses. When we are challenged to deal with a friend or family member with mental illness in any degree of depth, day-to-day life activities drastically change. Everyone in a relationship with the mentally ill person is afflicted in some way. Our original relationship with the person could now be very different. We must adjust to their behavior changes caused by bipolar disorder, schizophrenia, depression, etc. Today treatments are improving, but there is still a great need for improvement and better education about mental illness to reduce stigma. Mental illness can be absolutely devastating, and unless one has personally been engaged in this type of situation with family or friend, there is often no concept of the experience. In situations like this when we pray to God we can have faith that things are being accomplished. Perhaps someone cannot control their mental state, but we can to keep them in prayer because we want to see the person that we love come back and be at peace and in their right mind. A few related and powerful verses I have used many times include

Luke 1:37 "For no word from God will ever fail" (NIV).

Luke 18:27 "...What is impossible with man is possible with God" (NIV).

Ephesians 3:20 "Now to him who is able to do immeasurable more than all we ask or imagine, according to the power that is at work within us" (NIV).

It is good to stop and learn, to pick up another gem of grace, love and mercy. God is teaching us something!

When you have faced and overcome tragedy and tribulation, the next thing you may want to consider is helping someone in the same situation. You can do something like creating a fund or a support group, or you can serve others in simple ways like making them a meal, having their home or car cleaned, or getting them a AAA card so they have 365 day of protection of during travel. They might end up needing it and giving you a huge thank-you some day!

Wisdom Gained

Wisdom Gained

YELLOW LIGHT

YELLOW LIGHT

When I speak about 'yellow lights' in our lives, I am talking about situations in life where it is a bit harder to discern whether we should stay where we are or go forward. Let's consider how we feel when we see a traffic light change from green to yellow when we are driving. We may want to plow through regardless of the risks and dangers of doing so. When we stop for the yellow light we are anxious to take off to our destination as soon as that light changes. So many times I have gone ahead without enough consideration of the future or the possible consequences that could arise, only to find out I should have slowed down and used caution. This becomes very evident to me when the outcome I pursued didn't turn out the way I wanted it to.

A great scripture in the Bible is **John 16:13 "But when he, the Spirit of truth, comes, he will guide you into all truth. He will not speak on his own; he will speak only what he hears, and he will tell you what is yet to come" (NIV).** When I slow down and seek counsel and ask others to pray for me while I wait on God to show me what He wants me to do, things begin to move smoothly. Then when I have peace I know how to approach a situation, which may not be the original way I may have wanted to go. It is very dangerous to charge blindly ahead into a situation without wisdom, no relatable knowledge, or any type of feedback from others to consider. When we charge like a bull moose, the ending can be disastrous!

The Bible says that wisdom is worth more than rubies and gold. Did you know that gold goes through fire to remove impurities? I was at a conference once I heard a very profound statement. Someone said, "When God puts us in the fire, how do you think He knows when to pull us out? He knows His work is done when we are made pure and He sees His reflection in us!" Wow! Trials and tribulations are painful and difficult to endure, but there is a purpose! When we are not familiar with a situation, then it is even more important that we remain under God's protection, provision and power. **Roman 8:28 says "We know that in all things God works for the good of those who love him, who have been called according to his purpose" (NIV).**

One realizes that getting married is a profound situation when they consider the marriage vow to stay with their partner "for better or worse, for richer and poorer, till death do us part." It is important to be equally yoked with a person who believes the same things as you. This is ideal and a blessing. When a Christian is equally yoked with a Christian spouse who loves God, their relationship honors

God. An equally yoked couple will have a solid foundation and a joyful, true bond of love.

The phrase 'for richer or poorer' certainly sifts out those that are not in it for the long haul! I have had some very rough financial times and so have a few of my friends and family. We really know who our true friends are when these times appear! The other part of the marriage vow, 'till death do us part' is often not taken to heart; unfortunately, far too many couples throw in the towel before giving the marriage all they have. I do believe that in extreme situations, for example in the case of abuse that cannot be tolerated, there may exceptions when it is better for the couple to part. However, I am thankful and comforted we can know that our true friends, family and spouse will be there until our final breath.

We need to look with the eyes of caution when we have begun a relationship with someone. We need to look at the background of the person. We need to understand their desires, wants, expectations of us. We need all of God's power, provision and protection to connect in a healthy way. A relationship cannot work if it is does not match up with what we believe. This I can attest that I definitely have made wrong choices, gone down the wrong paths taken that led to dead ends The damage cannot be taken back. Because I didn't consider the possible outcomes and did not seek good counsel and encouragement from the spiritual word of God, my paths failed miserably.

We all need to be covered in prayer. We need to have people in our lives that pray over us for God's protection. Scripture reminds us that "No weapon formed against us will ever prosper." In other words, through prayer God will bring us through the firestorm we have created on our own. One verse that gives me strength when I have miserably failed is **Isaiah 54:17:" 'No weapon forged against you will prevail, and you will refute every tongue that** accuses you. This is the heritage of the servants of the Lord, and this is their vindication from me,' declares the Lord" (NIV).** I want to be under the protection of the Lord, full of the Holy Spirit. I want to feel His presence, and I want to be full of His assurance, filled with His scripture in my mind and heart. I want to say and do good things that will please Him.

The yellow light is powerful because we can stop, be alert, and rethink our direction. When facing a decision, we must ask ourselves "Is this beneficial? Is this going to bring a good outcome, or will it bring more of what I don't want: separation, abandonment, fear and anger?" **Proverbs 18:21** says **"the tongue has the power of life and death, and those who love it will eat its fruits" (NIV).** Have you ever said something that you later wished you hadn't said? I have interviewed dozens of people and not one person has ever said "no" to this question! We cannot go back to retrieve the hurtful words we have spoken in malice. We must be wise enough to never say them.

Galatians 5:22-23 "But the fruit of the Spirit is love, joy, peace, forbearance, kindness, goodness, faithfulness, gentleness and self-control. Against such things there is no law" (NIV).

Of all those fruits of the spirit, I consider self-control to be the bookend of them all. So many times I have remained silent through my tears. I control my mouth and keep silent as I imagine visions of my precious lord, king and master Jesus as He was on the cross, stabbed, mocked, beaten, spit upon, cut by a crown of thorns, nailed through His hands and feet, and whipped mercilessly. Yet through all that abuse, He never said one word to defend himself. My brain cannot conceive of the amazing love that Jesus had for his persecutors when He pleaded with God, saying "Father, Father, forgive them for they do not know what they do." I find it very interesting and helpful to remember Jesus' response during this painful ordeal. He took our sins on his shoulders and bore the penalty for the whole entire world's sin in silence. Our sins came upon the Lord, every single one we have made and will make. Jesus' sacrifice helps me to control myself not strike back at my abusers. **Philippians 2:3-5: "Do nothing out of selfish ambition or vain conceit. Rather, in humility value others above yourselves, not looking to your own interests but each of you to the interests of the others. In your relationships with one another, have the same mindset as Christ Jesus" (NIV).** Our attitude should be the same as that of Christ Jesus, even with our enemies. It will take a *full* portion of the Holy Spirit; nothing of the flesh can be in our person to truly love others.

I have learned that when I hold a certain idea about something and I share it with a person who has an opinion which complete opposes mine, they might turn on me or respond very violently and rudely. When this happens I should not be hostile or offended in turn. Instead, I try to respond respectfully and say something like 'That is interesting, I had never looked at it that way,' or, 'You have made a good point to consider.' Next time you are in such a situation, try these responses and see how the outcome will resolve in a more positive manner.

When you find yourself in a difficult situation, tensions are running high and you are not giving a peaceful response, take control of the situation. Stop and ask the other person, "Can we please reconnect in a few days, I need some time to think about your points,' or, 'I'll get back to you, let me put this together in my head; I need some more time to sort out my thoughts.' Most people will give you the time you need and they will also calm down and be more open with you. In a few days you will both be more calm and you both may share your input and ideas together more respectfully. In **Romans 12:3** Paul states, **"for by the grace given me I say to** every one of you; do not think of yourselves more highly than you ought, but rather think of yourself with sober judgment in accordance with the faith God has distributed to each of you" (NIV). I love this verse because it indicates the main things that we need to get along well with others are humbleness and thoughtfulness. Give grace to others as we have been given grace.

While sitting at a yellow light, we must wait for a green one to move forward. Likewise, even through our suffering we must stop and take precaution, and wait patiently for the green signal to go forward God tells Paul in **2 Corinthians 12:9a** that **"'My grace is sufficient for you, for my power is made perfect in weakness'" (NIV).** I don't like to be weak. I want to march on in power, driving forward full of God's wisdom, a soldier conquering for Him. However, it is in my weakest hour, when I seek God desperately, that I find God has graciously and sweetly broken me down to teach me to relinquish my will.

Jesus went asked his twelve disciples to pray for him because he knew what he would face and had deep anguish about his upcoming trial. Imagine if you had twelve close friends and went to them saying, "I have a life-and-death matter facing me and I need to pray. Will you keep watch and pray for me?" Jesus did this but returned three times to his disciples to find them sleeping each time. Can you imagine how you would feel when you found out your friends ignored your plea for help during such a desperate situation? During our most serious trials we find that we cannot lean on other people, but only on God. When we are going through a trial that He has put before us, we must do our best to be obedient and please him even when it seems almost impossible. On bent knees with tears in my eyes, I thank God on a daily basis that Jesus said,

"Not my will but yours will be done." A Christ-like mind is reflected in the following verses:

1 Corinthians 2:13 "This is what we speak, not in words taught us by human wisdom but in words taught by the Spirit, explaining spiritual realities with Spirit-taught words" (NIV).

1 Corinthian 2:16 "'Who has known the mind of the Lord so as to instruct him?' But we have the mind of Christ" (NIV).

Roman 12:2 "Do not conform to the pattern of this world, but be transformed by the renewing of your mind. Then you will be able to test and approve what God's will is—his good, pleasing and perfect will" (NIV).

Compassion, I have also learned, is the best gift to give when someone is suffering with a problem, a loss, or any stressful situation. Perhaps you have come upon a friend or stranger with tears in their eyes or they look distressed. The best response is to smile and let them know you are available and there for them. Don't drill them with questions or press for answers. They really just need to know you are there if and when they want to talk. Be a good listener. Listen and you will hear the needs of a person through their conversation. Knowing someone cares provides comfort and leeway for them to ask for what they need. I have learned when someone has suffered from a death of a loved one, it is best not to say "I know how you feel" if you really haven't been in the exact same situation. In their sadness they just need to know that you care. When most people are hurting they don't want people in their homes, they understandably desire to be alone for a while in their grief. Respect their privacy. Simply let them know you were thinking of them and care for them.

Remember that while we are practicing to use caution, we must also be ready and prepared to share the fruits of the spirit. Be full of the Holy Spirit and full of wisdom. **Proverbs 8:11** says **"For wisdom is more precious than rubies, and nothing you desire can compare with her" (NIV).** This especially applies if you are going into a business situation. Seek out wise input and ask many people with experience about any question that you may have. Ask for details of their experiences so that you can plan and have wisdom regarding the business you desire to enter. I have worked hard as a property manager, property owner, broker, and realtor. I have encouraged a number of people along the way simply because they asked me, "How did you get to where you are?"

I mentor other ladies and a few couples and I also have five women who mentor me and guide me. The good thing about my mentors is they vary in age. A few are up to a decade older than me and a few are up to a decade younger, which really allows for full exploration of the matter at hand from different perspectives. We should not go through life without support and help. God did not intend for us to live that way. The Bible continually tells us that we should seek wisdom, both from God and from other people that are wiser than us.

We should also seek wisdom when it comes to how we handle our finances and possessions. We can't take money with us when we die, but we sure don't live like it! I once saw a bumper sticker that said "the one that dies with the most toys wins." That could not be further from the truth! God wants our *hearts* first and foremost. When He has our hearts, He has our entire life and finances in His hands. When we live life understanding that everything we have belongs to God, it frees us. We don't have to live up to the expectations of other people around us. We don't have to keep up with the Joneses. We can live in a way that shows we depend on God. God takes care of the lilies of the field so will He take care of us. Appreciate and use the resources God has already given you for His glory. Praise God!

One time I was going through a very difficult financial situation. I was hungry and for breakfast I wanted two eggs. I decided that I should only have one egg because money was tight. When I cracked that one egg in the pan, there were two yolks! I started to laugh and cry at the same time because the yolk is my favorite part of the egg. Just this tiny reminder of God's love for me warmed my heart. God knows our every desire. Only God could have given me a double-yolked egg!

God came through for me another time when I was seriously lacking in finances. Somehow, an acquaintance coincidentally blessed me with the exact amount I needed to make the unpaid bills. Do you have any examples of your own of when God blessed you at the exact moment you needed a blessing? I bet you do!

A song I really love is called 'I Can Only Imagine'. It is about the day we will meet Jesus face to face. **Revelations 21:4** says **"'He will wipe every tear**

from their eyes. There will be no more death' or mourning or crying or pain, for the old order of things has passed away" (NIV). What a day that will be, when there are no more tears and we are walking on streets of gold! So in life, take time to stop and remember that after all the trials, our reward in heaven will be more than worth any suffering we endured on earth.

And that concludes the yellow light – Caution.

Wisdom Gained

Wisdom Gained

GREEN LIGHT

GREEN LIGHT

A green light means you should take your foot off the brake and step on the gas, it's time to go!

Psalm 23:2 "He makes me lie down in green pastures, he leads me beside quiet waters" (NIV).

Jeremiah 11:16 "The LORD called you a thriving olive tree with fruit beautiful in form. But with the roar of a mighty storm He will set it on fire, and its branches will be broken" (NIV).

Psalm 52:8 "But I am like an olive tree flourishing in the house of God; I trust in God's unfailing love forever and ever" (NIV).

Psalm 92:12-13 "The righteous will flourish like a palm tree, they will grow like a cedar of Lebanon;

planted in the house of the Lord, they will flourish in the courts of our God" (NIV).

Psalm 37:2 "For like the grass they will soon wither, like green plants they will soon die away" (NIV).

Genesis 1:30 "And to all the beasts of the earth and all the birds in the sky and all the creatures that move along the ground—everything that has the breath of life in it—I give every green plant for food." And it was so" (NIV).

This chapter about green lights is about recognizing when God wants you to move towards a blessing he has in store for you. I have chosen the verses above because they include imagery of the color green when they mention flourishing plant life. Green is a very important color for growth. In the Bible, green represents life, prosperity, new beginnings, freshness, and resting in the peace and tranquility of the knowledge of God. Green is the most restful color for the human eye, and looking at it can improve vision. Green is associated with durability, endurance, wealth, increase, nature, fertility, and safety. Olive green represents peace and tranquility, something that we all need. I myself am partial to green because the Lord blessed me with vibrant green eyes!

It is amazing when we take a moment to look out at nature. The beautiful green grass, the green trees, and the green mountains are all God's handiwork. I really believe that a tree is a wonderful gift to give someone. A friend of mine had a mother who loved the dogwood tree. When my friend's mother passed, I gave my friend a dogwood tree in her mother's honor, and it is now growing on their property as a memorial. I recommend that you plant a tree for your child or someone in the family. Commemorate the day you planted it and document the growth of the tree along with the child to celebrate their own growth. It is fun, unique, and special, and a gift that will last for years

Jeremiah 17:8 "They will be like a tree planted by the water that sends out its roots by the stream.

It does not fear when heat comes; its leaves are always green. It has no worries in a year of drought and never fails to bear fruit" (NIV).

Ezekiel 17:24 "'All the trees of the forest will know that I the Lord bring down the tall tree and make the low tree grow tall. I dry up the green tree and make the dry tree flourish. I the Lord have spoken, and I will do it'" (NIV).

Psalm 34:4 "I sought the Lord, and he answered me; he delivered me from all my fears" (NIV).

Philippians 4:6-7 "Do not be anxious about anything, but in every situation, by prayer and petition, with thanksgiving, present your requests to God. And the peace of God, which transcends all understanding, will guard your hearts and your minds in Christ Jesus" (NIV).

1 Peter 5:6-7 "Humble yourselves, therefore, under God's mighty hand, that he may lift you up in due

time. Cast all your anxiety on him because he cares for you" (NIV).

Psalm 55:22-23 "Cast your cares on the Lord and he will sustain you; He will never let the righteous be shaken" (NIV).

Proverbs 12:25 "Anxiety weighs down the heart, but a kind word cheers it up" (NIV).

Matthew 6:25-27 "'Therefore I tell you, do not worry about our life, what you will eat or drink; or about your body, what you will wear... Look at the birds of the air; they do not sow or reap or store away in barns, and yet our heavenly Father feeds them. Are you not much more valuable than they? Can any of you by worrying add a single hour to your life?'" (NIV).

Philippians 4:13 "I can do all this through him who gives me strength" (NIV). One of my friends, a young girl, asked for prayer. I prayed for her for many days, sometimes with her and sometimes by myself on my own. She later confided in me that almost everything I did irritated her. As I gently pressed her for further information she told me she didn't like the way I prayed. I said, "Really? Let me tell you a story about the oyster." I explained to her that when a grain of sand enters an oyster, the small grain irritates the oyster's inner tissues. The oyster secretes a liquid upon the grain of sand, layer by layer. Those layers of liquid harden, and eventually that tiny irritating grain of sand turns into a beautiful cultured pearl. I said that my words to her were like a grain of sand that irritated an oyster, but that God was using me to make a pearl out of her! She really loved that analogy. The next day she called me and asked me to go to a luncheon with her. When she initially shared her feelings with me, I had been hurt, but through the grace of God I was able to be kind, gentle and humble in my response. I could not have been so if I didn't have Jesus' word in my heart and mind. Through growing in Jesus myself, my spirit was green and full of life and hope, not death. I did not let her words hurt me, but instead used the love of God to spread life and hope to her.

I once attended a three-month class regarding grieving and death. It helped immensely. My father died when I was three and my mother died when I was eleven, but I didn't realize that I had never fully processed the grief of losing them. As a young girl I learned not to talk, trust, or feel emotion; I needed to take care of everybody else. As an adult, that mindset of 'others first' prevented me from having any authentic happiness or freedom. After learning about how to deal with grief and anxiety I could finally release it. Anxiety and grief in a soul are like a steam in pressure cooker. The pressure needs to be released! Now that my spirit is no longer full of negativity, I can grow in spiritual gifts like love, kindness, openness and compassion. Sometimes I notice that a friend or family member has a bit of stress or anxiety, and that they are being unkind to me because of their own unpleasant feelings. To show them I care, I'll do something cute like send a little notecard with a toothpick attached to it and write, "Please stop picking on me!" It diffuses tension and helps them laugh. I get a good response from others when I give them that card. They appreciate that I was gentle in expressing my feelings to them. Send words of encouragement and lift up others when they are feeling low. You will both grow!

1 Corinthians 2:9-10 "However, as it is written: 'What no eye has seen, what no ear has heard, and what no human mind has conceived' - the things God has prepared for those who love him— these are the things God has revealed to us by his Spirit. The Spirit searches all things, even the deep things of God" (NIV).

2 Corinthians 4:16 "Therefore we do not lose heart. Though outwardly we are wasting away, yet inwardly we are being renewed day by day" (NIV).

Now I don't know about you, but there are many people I talk to who are ready for the new body we will receive in Heaven right now! I know I am ready as I have a few wrinkles and rolls myself! A new body is something to look forward to. Meanwhile, as I wait on the Lord's return, I juice raw fruits and vegetables and eat lots of leafy greens to maintain my earthly body the best that I can.

This first miracle that Jesus ever performed was to turn water into wine at his mother's request. The wine that Jesus made was better than the first wine that had been served! That reminds me that we should give the best gifts we can to others. When we give a gift something to somebody, we should give it graciously. We shouldn't present it as something being discarded or unwanted or say anything negative about it. Give with kindness and love. The person receiving it will receive it with love. For example, when I share an orange with my friend, I cut it in half and offer them the bigger half. It is the kind thing to do. Although I want the bigger half, I offer the bigger and better portion to my friend. The challenge arises when you have to share something you really enjoy like a chocolate chip cookie. In this case, the person who breaks it in half shouldn't get to choose which half they get, the other person does. This makes it fun too!

When we have come to a green light, we should feel relieved. I hope that you have profited from reading this analogy of how life is like a road with red, yellow and green traffic lights. No one has a perfect life, but when we are in Heaven and walking on streets of gold without fear, anxiety, tribulation or suffering, we will be home. Is the journey worth it? Absolutely! We need to finish the journey!! If we fall, we need to get back up. It doesn't matter how we get to the finish line or whether we walk, run, fall, stumble, or crawl. Always persevere! Hang in there, seek help, be kind to others, and take good care of yourself too.

One day on the telephone prayer line I participate in, one person asked the other listeners "what would you want to be said about you at your funeral?" I thought about that for three weeks! The answer finally came to me. After the day the good Lord takes me and my friends and family are at my funeral, I hope that the pastor will say, "Many knew Edith Dolores Roman. Her life wasn't easy. She was knocked down many times, and sometimes she felt like staying down. It was like she was knocked down in a boxing match and only had ten counts to get back up and fight, or she would lose the match. She almost surrendered, but at the count of ten she could hear the loud voice of God saying firmly, 'Get up Edith.' Bloody, beaten, and bruised, she reached for the ropes once again and got back up to be victorious. Today her last request is that any of you who would like know God on a deeper level or any of you who need a renewing of your walk with the Lord would please in a quiet voice repeat this Prayer of Salvation to our Lord and Savior:

> *'Father, I know that I have broken your laws and my sins have separated me from you. I am truly sorry, and now I*

want to turn away from my past sinful life toward you. Please forgive me, and help me avoid sinning again. I believe that your son, Jesus Christ died for my sins, was resurrected from the dead, is alive, and hears my prayer. I invite Jesus to become the Lord of my life, to rule and reign in my heart from this day forward. Please send your Holy Spirit to help me obey You, and to do Your will for the rest of my life. In Jesus' name I pray, Amen.'"

So, it is with love, prayers, and much respect that I ask you to do your best in applying the lessons of this book to learn, change and help others. I am honored that you have taken the time to read it. I pray that you will share it with many and that it will help to bring you the peace, tranquility, joy and happiness that you certainly deserve. Amazing grace has now begun with a green light. Amen.

Wisdom Gained

Wisdom Gained

Red

Your experiences on the red light to stop in your tracks.

Yellow

Your experiences as you waited for information or prayed through it.

Green

When you took your foot off your break the green light, what were your experiences that you capture through the 911 problem and what could you give back to a broken world from your experience.

Testimony 1

Bless the Lord, O my soul, and forget not all of his benefits (Psalms 103:2).

A Precious Jewel

That is exactly what friendship is, A Precious Jewel from God. My wife and I arrived in Santa Maria, CA over two years ago. Little did we know that God had a fiery young lady by the name of Edith Roman awaiting our arrival. From the moment we met until this present moment we have cherished our God given friendship.

This reminds me of David, when he arrived with Saul from battle. Jonathan, Saul's son, fell in love with David. Not that there was a hidden agenda, but Jonathan recognized God's anointing and presence with David. These were some of the very first words spoken by Sister Edith, "God has anointed you." She has shown love to us when really she did not have to. We love her dearly and cherish every moment we have with her, for she is precious to us.

Friends know how and when to bless you without you asking them. Often people do not know the value of a priceless jewel, until they discover the valuable dimensional depths of the jewel. Sister Edith will attend our church services at different times without our knowledge that she would be attending. On special occasions she will be there praising the Lord. There are times when my wife and I will be attending a special event and we will call Sister Edith and invite her to join us. Friends just enjoy the company of a friend.

Sister Edith, you are our friend and Sister in the Lord. God bless you and we love you.

Rev. Dr. Donald R. Wesson, Pastor/Teacher

What gift of wisdom did you receive from this testimony? ☆

How did this person turn their scars into stars? ☆

Testimony 2

Blended, Not Shaken...

Bruce and I had gathered with some close friends soon after returning from a sunburned Jamaican honeymoon. Following a beautiful dinner and lots of reminiscing, a friend told me that they overheard another wedding attendee say, "they won't make it a year." While it was true we were combining our families and had a rough road head of us, we were determined our love was strong enough and resilient. Nevertheless, we were somewhat outraged and disturbed at the negative comment. In retrospect and looking back over the years, it was God and our faith that pulled us through so many internal and external battles, teenage upheavals, former spouses, work that pulled one or the other of us away for periods of time, the four children's various school requirements and activities, shared parenting/custody struggles, continued court battles, and our own parents' needs pulling at both of us. It was an endless barrage of arrows flying hard and furious at us. Sometimes we were so shaken from all the craziness. We more often than not went back to the basics to regroup, God's word.

Guess what? We are celebrating our 25th anniversary this year. We made it! Quite well, thank you. In retrospect we believe we made it because God facilitated our growth in our faith through the trials and joys. We prayed for each other and our children. We both practiced lots of forgiveness, practicing what God taught us to do. We treated each other's children as our own and tried to be fair in all our interactions and decisions. We were united in our decisions and backed each other up. Here is our hold-tight-to-scripture verse; we hope it gives you encouragement, joy, comfort, and hope as you blend your families together too.

> **Romans 12:9-13 (NIV)** - *Love must be sincere. Hate what is evil; cling to what is good. Be devoted to one another in love. Honor one another above yourselves. Never be lacking in zeal, but keep your spiritual fervor, serving the Lord. Be joyful in hope, patient in affliction, and faithful in prayer. Share with the Lord's people who are in need. Practice hospitality.*

Bruce and Kelley Williams

What gift of wisdom did you receive
from this testimony? ☆

How did this person turn their scars into stars? ☆

Testimony 3

Romans 8:31 (NIV) - *If God is for us, who can be against us?*

Hello, my name is Aleesha Klomp. I am thirty-six years old. I am a mother of two beautiful children named Jocelynn, who's eleven, and Gryphon, who's nine. I have been married for fifteen years to my wonderful and loving husband Michael.

Edie and I met at a women's Bible study in Shell Beach, CA. We have since become friends who share many moments. Our favorite time to share together involves Edie making organic popcorn and myself bringing the candy bars. We love seeing movies together and laughing. We have been able to share special prayer times together. WE have also been able to stand in prayer for one another through some tough times. I am really thankful for my friendship with Edie and I will continue to pray God blesses her in everything she does.

I wanted to share a story with you about some of the struggles I have endured in my life over the years. When my daughter was about a year and a half, I noticed she had several bruises on her legs that weren't healing. I took her into our physician, who ran a few blood tests. We later found out Jocelynn was a carrier of a rare blood disorder called ITP. Basically inside our bodies we have blood cells that clot to help us stop bleeding when we hurt ourselves. Jocelynn unfortunately had a lower amount of these, so I was instructed to watch her very carefully. If Jocelynn fell or hurt herself, there was a possibility of her bleeding internally.

Now this blood disorder was rare, but it was also untreatable. Whenever I noticed broken blood vessels on her skin I would have to take her in to get her blood count ran to see if she was bleeding internally or not. Thankfully she never got to that point. My husband and I prayed every day for her healing. We saw God do an absolute miracle in her life. She outgrew this disorder by the age of five. We were so thankful!

Now our son was born when Jocelynn was almost three. His name is Gryphon. Gryphon was born as a full term, healthy baby. On his eighth day of life, Gryphon woke up and was the color of an apricot. I called his doctor and took Gryphon in to be seen. They sent me over to a hospital to have his labs drawn.

About eight hours later I received a phone call telling me to take Gryphon to an emergency room. My husband and I took him there and as soon as we arrived things began to get crazy. The doctors began strapping Gryphon down and giving him oxygen. They were trying to get in through his almost-healed belly button. We were told he was in critical condition. We waited about three hours and then were told he would need to be transferred to a children's hospital.

We later found out Gryphon almost died from a really high level of bilirubin in his system. The doctors had to give him a blood transfusion that removed and replaced eighty-five percent of his blood. Gryphon began to have seizures and ended up in the hospital for almost an entire month. When we were finally discharged from the hospital, Michael and I were told our son was completely deaf. He probably would never eat on his own, sit up on his own or do much of anything by himself. The doctors predicted our son to live in a vegetable-like state.

Over the course of the next year we were told Gryphon had cerebral palsy and a hearing disorder. He began many therapy programs and even stem cell injections in China. Gryphon is now nine years old and we continue to have struggles, but he is a strong, healthy, determined little boy who loves life. He can walk and eat and sit and stand and even run a little. He also can hear us and speak and he attends school. God has done a miracle in his life and continues to strengthen him and our family every day. We have turned our scars into stars with the help of our Lord Jesus Christ and we are so honored to love a God who never gives up on us!

THANK YOU!

Aleesha Klomp

What gift of wisdom did you receive from this testimony? ☆

How did this person turn their scars into stars? ☆

Testimony 4

I am so thankful to God for the many mentors, role models, and brothers and sisters in Christ that He has put in my life. I was blessed to meet Edith this year, and we immediately had a strong spiritual connection. As I grew to know her while I worked with her to edit her book and organize her office, she gave me a great deal of wisdom from her past decades of experience of walking with the Lord. She told me of struggling with abuse, poverty, and depression since when she was a child up through her adulthood. However, at the same time as I was learning about her life challenges, I was going through the papers in her office and I kept finding newspaper articles extolling this amazing woman Edith Roman, who had surprised so many people by becoming a young and successful real estate agent against all odds. Her stories of intense hardship often shocked me, but her testimony and success encouraged me that no matter what mistreatment we endure, no matter what hardships we encounter, no matter how the enemy attacks us, Jesus is our refuge, our rock, and our salvation.

Edith taught me about the five spiritual gifts - Encouragement, Gifts, Acts of Service, Quality Time, and Touch. Each of us has a specific gift or gifts that are a primary way that we like to show love to others. Edith and I both share the gift of encouragement. I encourage her to hold onto her optimism and achieve her goals when she is being discouraged, and she encourages me to be wise, faithful, and humble. She reminds me that I need to have Godly standards, not worldly standards, because I am a "Woman of Excellence." I am grateful for her continual admonishments for me to leave my pride out of situations so that the grace of God can heal all hurts and have the victory.

I feel that the connection between Edith and I has a supernatural aspect to it that is shown in the similarity of our spirits and minds. So many times Edith and I have read each others' thoughts and completed each others' sentences. Even phrases, verses, or songs will come up in my life for me that relate to a recent conversation or experience I shared with her. Just the other night when I was talking to her about writing this note for her book, I looked at my digital clock twice, exactly at 8:28 and 9:11. This was so important to me because just last month on August 28, I had sent Edith a message wishing her a "Happy 8/28 Day," because her last name is Roman and one of my favorite power verses is Romans 8:28: "And we know that in all things God works for the good of those who love Him, who are called according to his purpose." Also, the term "9-1-1" is one that Edith often uses to signify an emergency situation, or a "red light," as she says in this book. I thank God for these reminders that serve as confirmation for me that the relationship between Edith and I is an anointed one. I have been blessed to know her and I pray that others who are seeking encouragement in their life are blessed to find someone else who encourages them not only to persevere, but to respond to the challenges and trials of their life with optimism, integrity, and grace.

I have come to know for myself how God works in mysterious ways. Every day I am increasingly thankful for the ways in which I see His hand orchestrate the events of my life. At the age of 27 I already have experienced how God can humble or exalt me, and how no matter what He puts before me, it will be to serve His glorious purpose. From my early childhood years as an introverted and awkward bookworm to blossoming in high school to be a cross-country runner and make friends, from struggling with stress in college to finally graduate with a degree from Stanford, from contending with depression and enduring manic episodes when trying to drop an antidepressant to being returned to a sane mind, joyfulness, and being medication-free, I know from my own personal experiences that God takes us through the valleys and mountains to train us to always stick close to Him. Right now I am the happiest I have ever been in my life, and I know it was because I made a choice on November 6, 2014 to let go of the one thing holding me back in my relationship with Jesus. I am completely amazed at my transformation over the past year. After deciding to give absolutely everything to God, my economic, health, and relationship situations may have fluctuated, but my joy and appreciation for my life has steadily increased. I am finally learning to be like Job: "Though he slay me, yet will I hope in him" (Job 13:15). With the last ten months I lost my job, broke my ankle, needed a root canal, and my car engine was ruined after I followed some bad advice to drive it rather than have it towed. I'll admit that my initial responses to these situations were discouragement and frustration, but I have been able to find the good in all of them. After I lost my job I had more free time to go to the lunchtime prayer meetings and weekday services at my church, and started to go to as many as I could every week, so I praise God that I was fired because it was the catalyst for my spiritual rejuvenation. After healing from my broken ankle I more appreciated being able-bodied and began running on a regular basis, much more than I had before I was injured. When I needed a root canal I was thankful to God that I was able to get last-minute COBRA dental coverage (with only about a ten days left to enroll in it), that my father was able to help me pay for the procedure, and that I lived in a place where I had access to such dental services at all. After not being able to use my car I took advantage of carpooling with friends and enjoying the conversations we had on drives, and I returned to longboarding, one of my favorite hobbies that I hadn't engaged in for months. I truly began to know, not just say, that God is always good. He is good indeed, and He has put a fire in my heart to tell as many people as I can about his goodness. My joy and strength is in JESUS. So every day I wear my ring engraved with Philippians 4:13 as a reminder: "I can do all things through Christ who gives me strength."

Ogochukwu Agbo

What gift of wisdom did you receive from this testimony? ☆

How did this person turn their scars into stars? ☆

Testimony 5

Matthew 5:46: "If you love *only those who love you, what reward is there for you?*"

I have known Edie and had a friendship with her for the last five years and it started out great. The friendship got a little rocky at times. We still continued to visit and attended church occasionally. It was clear that God had this friendship for His will to be glorified and to love the difficult in each other! This refreshes my mind about the verse, Matthew 5:46 "If you love only those who love you, what reward is there for you? It was extremely obvious that after running into Edie at the movies, hardware store, supermarket and a Christmas Play at a church that neither one of us attended there was no question that these were supernatural encounters that we had no control over. At these places we were cordial and exchanged a few words and moved on. It was truly amazing and I sent an email inviting Edie to a Young Living educational class on Essential Healing Oils taught by Lisa. Edie then contacted Lisa convinced it was definitely a mistake on Shirley's part. Without going into details, Edie asked Lisa to confirm this invitation to assure the invitation was truly intended. And sure enough Lisa called Edie back and said she would be delighted to have you attend the class. I have seen tremendous transformations, to the glory of God, and Edie is a mighty intercessor, warrior, hears from God and obeys. She also mentors many couples and people of many cultures.

I would highly recommend that you read Turning Your Storms into Rainbows. I even had a dream that she was honored and lifted up at this up Christian meeting we had and hundreds of people were there and it was to demonstrate the great changes and what God had done in her life. Many old past patterns have now diminished to the glory of God. She is a brand-new woman of God.

We now share a beautiful relationship with laughter joy, healthy recipes, breaking bread together and our young living essential oils business. The fruits of the Spirit are now present in our relationship. Galatians 5:22 -23: "But the fruit of the Spirit is love, joy, peace, forbearance, kindness, goodness, faithfulness, gentleness and self-control against which there is no law."

Shirley Chandlerk

What gift of wisdom did you receive from this testimony? ☆

How did this person turn their scars into stars? ☆

Testimony 6

My name is Diana Jones. Edith Roman is my foster sister. My parents started taking in foster children when I was about 12 years old. My parents had gotten a 10-month old baby girl about a year before I got married, whom they later adopted. Later, Edie came to live at my parents' house when I had been married about a year or so. Edi seemed to fit right in with the family. She always had a smile on her face. My mother and my older sister Irene got along very well with Edie. My mom started teaching Edie about homemaking and preparing for her adult years. When Edie was in high school and getting ready for her prom, my mom asked me if I would make Edie's prom dress. When I was in high school I had taken sewing and made my own prom dress besides many other dresses. My mom asked me if I was up for the challenge and I agreed. Edie has never forgotten, so I guess she approved of my sewing skills. She was very pleased with her dress and went off to prom with her boyfriend Francisco.

As years passed, I moved a few times and lost track of Edie. Around 1983 my mom had a stroke and Edie got in touch with me as she was very upset. My mom had gone into a rest home where she passed about two years later. I again lost touch with Edie. Many years had passed and my older sister Irene had mentioned that we should try to locate her. We both wanted to see her again. In 2010 my sister Irene became ill and passed away. Remembering my sister's wish of trying to find Edie, I had my daughter Brenda search for her, and sure enough she found her. I was so excited and when I called Edie, and I knew she was as excited as I was. We have been telephone corresponding for the past 5 years. One of these days we will see each other again in person. I always have a good time when I chat with Edie on the telephone. She has a very positive outlook on life and never has a bad word to say about anyone. She still remembers the prom dress I made for her. We always have fun talking to each other.

When Edie was living with my parents, my mother got an award for Mother of the Year from the foster society. There was an article and a picture of our mom with Edie and my younger sister that my parents had adopted in the paper. I happened to come across that newspaper article and picture not too long ago and gave it to Edie. I felt she should have it as a memory keepsake of her and our mother.

Edie is an absolute treasure and I cherish our 2-hour talks. We always say we will cut our talks shorter, but it always seems like we have a lot to talk about, and it's always positive.

Edie doesn't feel like my foster sister, she is just my sister, and I love her dearly. This is dedicated to our mother and sister Irene. I know they felt the same way about Edie as I do. They loved her as I do. We love you Edie!!!!!!!!!!!!

Diana Jones

What gift of wisdom did you receive from this testimony? ☆

How did this person turn their scars into stars? ☆

Testimony 7

I've known Edie for about a year now. A mutual friend, George Barnes, introduced us, and she began attending our church, and finally became a part of our church family.

Quickly, I discovered that Edie was a very special Christian. Her desire to share her faith, and be an encourager was crystal clear to me. Her strong faith radiates in everything she does. Many times I saw myself inadequate to match her positive spirit, and radiating optimism.

Early on, her passion to serve led to a misunderstanding. I feared we would lose her after we pointed out how things get done in our church. I made some mistakes in failing to be up front with her about such matters when she became a part of our family. I didn't want to lose her. I knew we had someone very gifted. We talked, and she stayed. She overlooked my failings and saw how much my wife, Linda, and I love and adore her.

Her passion for other's welfare is contagious. She invites her friends to come to worship, and she prays for everyone in need. She reaches out to help anyone she can. Having read her first book, "Turning Your Storms into Rainbows," I can tell you firsthand, she lives what she writes. I can't wait to read this book.

Edie's tragic childhood, serious accident, her many setbacks, painful experiences and her Christian faith make her more than qualified to write her two books. Anyone who read the first book will want to read her second. This precious Christian lady has an amazing head and heart full of wisdom that comes down from above. Open her books, open your heart and you will grow wiser.

An appropriate verse that reminds me of Edie is this: "The things you have learned and received and heard and seen in me, practice these things, and the God of peace will be with you" Philippians 4:9 (NAU).

Edie, I love you and will be looking for a third book from you soon! You have blessed my life beyond measure!

Rob Redden, Minister and friend.

Testimony 8

I met Edie by the power of the "Holy Spirit"! My name was on a list and she picked me out to have an appointment with me. Edie has prayed with me, cried with me and laughed with me. Whenever I need some sound advice and some spiritual uplifting I can always count on Edie. She has been there through thick and thin. She is a woman of God and always stays balanced with all of the crazy things happening in this world. She is a true friend!

Michael Hunstad
Senior Loan Officer

What gift of wisdom did you receive from this testimony? ☆

How did this person turn their scars into stars? ☆

Testimony 9

Edith Roman is the constant disciple, learning and being an unselfish friend at every turn in life. Edith is a sound Christian author of two very motivating books; "Turning Your Storms into Rainbows" and "Turning your Scars into Stars," and is relentless in her efforts to help motivate others.

Edith was a student at the Barnes Institute of Management Productivity through several courses, manuscript and speech and communication skills and always finishing at the top of the class.

Edith's spiritual behavior, loyal friendship and her positive attitude in life is contagious. Edith cares and is concerned for others, is willing to help others and displays esprit de corps actions in all her efforts, job wise and on a personal level of interacting with others.

Edith is well focused on all that she is involved in and works toward a positive and complete finish in fulfilling her assignments.

Turning your Scars into Stars is a very thought provoking book where the reader immediately understands the author's intent to help solve life problems. Understanding simple solutions to our personal life problems becomes simpler, even by the motivational title of Turning your Scars into Stars. Readers will be alerted and made conscious of what they can do for life's self help solutions. This writing will build a motivational platform and foundation structured with strength to clearly aid your mental awareness of what joy life has in store for you. The reader will be constantly enthused to elevate their vision for self improvement.

The author "Edith" guides the reader through a pathway of understanding of how to get solutions and positive actions to work for everyday happiness in life. Edith writes with a leadership manner, certainty and clarity enabling you to be self motivating and to take charge of life's problems and turn the scars into stars. In Edith's previous book "Turning Storms into Rainbows" a similar manner of understanding of how life can be made most pleasant is taught.

Edith is clearly spiritually guided in her writings and demonstrates an unselfish ability to be of help to others. Sometimes we are merely off track in our lives and need a simple resetting. There are times when more knowledge is of course more powerful. The author's leadership ability helps us to understand and take necessary action "without reservation" towards building a happier life and turning our scars into stars.

George Barnes
Founder and President
The Barnes Institute
Of Management Productivity

What gift of wisdom did you receive
from this testimony? ☆

How did this person turn their scars into stars? ☆

Testimony 10

In her first book, Turning Your Storms into Rainbows, and in this second book, Turning Your Scars into Stars, Edith Roman shares her experience in life rooted in the belief that Sacred Scripture is God's wisdom for all of humanity. Using the metaphor of a stop light with its Red, Yellow, and Green Light. She imparts her own wisdom of living life with all its ups and downs, trials and tribulations, joys and sufferings, with a sense of peace that surpasses all understanding. To the non-believer these words can be read as wisdom to guide you through all that life brings you. To the believer, those who are followers of their Creator, who seek God's guidance for direction in life, this book will provide guidance. Psalm 119:105 tells us that God's Word is a lamp, a light that illuminates the darkness. God's Word illuminates the path of our lives. If we keep God's Word shining along the way, then we will be far less likely to trip and fall. We will not be easily deceived. Because we are following the light, we will see what the light reveals in the path ahead of us. It is only when we turn the light off, before we have arrived at our destination, something could spring up in the dark and trip us.

Edith Roman will share God's light from Scripture with the wisdom and truth that will keep the light of God's truth shining brightly ahead of us. The stop light metaphor, in each major book section, reveals a lifetime of experience. The story is coupled with the wisdom she has learned, in her walk with the Lord, illuminated by Scripture and through prayer. As the Psalmist says, the symbolism of light or a lamp is used to show direction or instruction as a result of understanding God's Word. In other words, we can walk and live life imitating Jesus Christ because light and truth are given to him. In this book you will see that Jesus Christ was more than just the Light of Israel, as was said of Yahweh in Isaiah, Jesus is the light that gives light to everyone.

As Edith exhorts us, turn to prayer, don't let darkness rule your life, learn the points in life (Red Light, Yellow Light, Green Light) that cry out for wisdom and truth. "In him was life, and that life was the light of all people. The light shines in the darkness, and the darkness has not overcome it...The true light that gives light to everyone was coming into the world" (John 1:4-9).

Trent Benedetti is a financial planner and accountant. His counseling includes Biblical wisdom as the guide for right decision making. He has been providing his services in the Central Coast of California for over 33 years. He is the father of four, grandfather of four, and has been married to his wife, Barbara, for over 38 years.

What gift of wisdom did you receive from this testimony? ☆

How did this person turn their scars into stars? ☆

Testimony 11

A Faithful, Committed Women of God, My Friend
~ Edith Roman

First of all I would like to say that I am humbled that Sister Roman would ask me to introduce her. She is a humble servant, a renowned author, a mentor, a prayer warrior, a friend, and she loves Jesus Christ with ALL of her heart. She displays her love for Christ by helping, loving, encouraging the broken hearted, the hurting, and the wounded.

Her heart's desire is that all would be saved according to 1 Timothy 2:3&4, which says: " For this is good and acceptable in the sight of God our Saviour; (4) Who will have all men to be saved, and to come unto the knowledge of the truth." (KJV)

I first met Edith at a women's meeting in Santa Maria, Ca. That was the beginning of our friendship. Sister Roman has faced many trials and tribulations in her own life, and that is how her first book, "Turning your Storms into Rainbows" was birthed.

If you have ever been hurt, broken, misunderstood, or just need to be encouraged, or need a good spiritual read, I highly recommend "Turning your Scars into Stars." As you read this book, you will realize God is not a respecter of person. If he did it for Sister Roman, myself, and a multitude of others, HE WILL DO IT FOR YOU. As Sister Roman puts it, "What shall we then say to these things? If God be for us, who can be against us?" Romans 8:31. (KJV)

In Christ's Love,

Mary Reneau

What gift of wisdom did you receive from this testimony? ☆

How did this person turn their scars into stars? ☆

Testimony 12

Dear Edith:

Chapter 1 of Turning Your Storms into Rainbows by Edith Dolores Roman was entitled "Spiritual." It touched my heart, my soul and my spirit. In the inner being I delight in God's law. Romans 7:22

After reading just one chapter of Turning Your Storms Into Rainbows, I know my spiritual walk is strengthened and my joy in the Lord is renewed on a daily basis. I have been saved since the age of 16, when I asked Jesus to come into my heart and my life. Now, at the age of 60, I had not probed the scriptures and studied the Word as I now do every time I read a few pages of this book. This book has encouraged me to savor and study the

Word (The Holy Bible) and bask in God's plans for my life. I now record in my journal my favorite scriptures and dedicate them to memory and can recall God's words when I need to apply them to my life or to help someone else. I am praying more daily, sharing more Jesus daily. I want to be more like Jesus and make him known, and I want to be all that Jesus wants me to be and serve him with all that I am. Thank you Jesus for all that you are to me! Thank you Jesus for saving me! Thank you Lord for all that you have blessed me with. Lord I love you and I praise your holy name.

Sharon A. Youngblood

What gift of wisdom did you receive from this testimony? ☆

How did this person turn their scars into stars? ☆

Testimony 13

Edie and I, Dorothy Yelda, age 91 years, mother of 10 children, grandmother of 7, great-grandmother of 4, first met at a Family-to-Family education workshop sponsored by the Alliance for the Mentally Ill. At this workshop we discussed all the problems that parents encounter in dealing with those of our loved ones who have a mental illness. It was Edie who suggested that we meet on a weekly basis to discuss our problems and give support to each other after the workshop education was completed. The group gradually dissolved, but Edie and I continued to become fast friends, phoning frequently. "GOD BLESS" was how we ended our phone calls. We became acquainted with her son, and she became acquainted with some of my children. We gradually became aware of her deep faith in the Lord, praying with us on occasions. Her knowledge of biblical chapters and verses was refreshing. GOD BLESS!

Dorothy Yelda

What gift of wisdom did you receive from this testimony? ☆

How did this person turn their scars into stars? ☆

Testimony 14

Sister Edith (as I call her) is a true woman of God and the definition of "dignity and integrity". Her heart shines through her work and will penetrate your heart and soul. It will give you a desire to truly reach out to others and lead them on the path of righteousness just as Sister Edith so diligently does.

Melissa Rich

What gift of wisdom did you receive
from this testimony? ☆

How did this person turn their scars into stars? ☆

Testimony 15

I have known Edie Roman for two decades. We met at a church that neither of us now attends because of differing perspectives on doctrine and other personal issues that caused both of us to depart from the denomination of our spiritual rebirth. In addition, I have lived in South Florida for the last 11 years while Edie has remained on the Central Coast of California, yet we have retained our friendship over the years despite distance and time. Christ is the bond that has cemented our relationship.

In addition to differences in location and religious affiliations, Edie and I also share ethnic and age differences. I am African American woman who is 9 months older than her first born son. Edie is a White woman who is only 5 years younger than my mother. However, we have shared the bond of sisterhood that does not exhibit a maternal/subordinate relationship that one would expect in a world filled with racial tension that causes division. We have maintained our sisterhood through telephone conversations and prayer.

Edie and I have shared wonderful memories together. Edie was my realtor when I purchased a 3 unit property in Northern California-one that I still own today. Edie has stayed in my home when she drove up to the Bay Area to help another friend sell her home. Edie slept on my very uncomfortable sofa bed for nearly 2 weeks without complaining while at the same time serving me and my family by providing dinner and doing our laundry. I did not realize how uncomfortable that sofa was until I needed to sleep on it because my bed was being shipped to Florida. She had such a servant spirit that she kept the discomfort to herself and thanked me for the opportunity to stay with me. I can go on and on about the various events that we have shared together, but I won't because this letter would be way too long!

I will conclude with the fact that this past May my boyfriend and I visited Edie while we were visiting other family and friends in California. It was like 11 years of not seeing each other made no difference at all. Time a part had not changed our relationship! I am very happy that Edie is writing another book. Edie's life experiences have helped me and I am certain that by reading her new book other lives will be positively affected.

Lea Murray

What gift of wisdom did you receive from this testimony? ☆

How did this person turn their scars into stars? ☆

Testimony 16

Dear People of God,

Several years ago the Lord gave me an e-mail ministry. I felt a need to create a way to truly follow up on verbal commitments I would make to pray for friends and relatives. How many of you listen to a friend that is going through a tough situation and you feel for them and say, "I will truly pray for you"? You end the call or the contact with a prayer on your heart until maybe the baby cries or it is time for the next conference call and you do not think about the situation again because of your busy schedule.

Well, I became very burdened with my inability to follow up with a sincere prayer, so I started listing the prayer requests and publishing them every

Tuesday via email to a group of personal friends that were also "Prayer Warriors."

Over the years, I have met many people, whom I have added to the distribution list and the number of 'Prayer Warriors' has multiplied. However, with the increase in "junk" mail that is received via email, the Lord has led me to establish a website and allow people to submit their requests and come into our virtual prayer room.

God has taken our prayer team to another level. Utilizing technology, we have an open prayer line that women are free to join us Monday - Friday 6:15AM - 7:00AM (Pacific Standard TIme). On Fridays we invite guests such as men, women, and/or youth to speak or join in.

Over the years I have been honored to meet many special women and Edith Roman ranks among the precious circle of women. She listens to the call daily and prays over the requests. She engages in the teachings and she has also on several occasions led us in an anointed prayer. She taught a lesson on the five love languages from a biblical perspective and she shared a powerful message on the folded napkin.

She is a mother that prays consistently for her children and she brings all her issues to the Lord in prayer. She truly believes that God will transform her Scars to Stars she is a bright star waiting and believing in God's promises. I thank God for her first book Turning Your Storms Into Rainbows. She is an anointed woman of God.

Please feel free to join our prayer line any morning. The number is a toll number, so you may want to consider using your cell phone unless you have "unlimited" long distance service. If you miss the call, you can call 712-432-1085 access code 758894 to listen to the recorded call and the recording is replaced daily.

"Prayer Warriors For Life"

Connie McGrue

What gift of wisdom did you receive
from this testimony? ☆

How did this person turn their scars into stars? ☆

Testimony 17

"A friend loves at all times, and a brother is born for a time of adversity" Proverbs 17:17 (NIV)

I met Edith, a new loving friend, at an afternoon ballroom dance. We were sitting at the same table and I, Elvira, mentioned that I give ukulele and Hawaiian dance lessons. As I was leaving, Edith handed me a card and asked me to please let her know when I was giving another lesson. I called Edith and told her the lessons were Friday at 2:00 and sure enough she showed up. She had never played the Ukulele or danced Hawaiian, so we were in for a lot of work. By the end of the first lesson we found that we had more than the lessons in common. We enjoyed praying, cooking, and eating together. Edith shared with me that she had be praying for a spiritual mother and she was excited to spend time with me because she had lost her mom at a young age and she felt a mother/daughter bond with me.

The more we met the closer we got. We shared the good and bad in our lives, we laughed a lot and cried a lot. I enjoyed teaching her and seeing her being excited about it and I was repaid with her helping me buy my first smartphone, a big and exciting event for a 91 year young woman.

When Edith found out when my birthday was, she asked me with great excitement what my favorite cake was. I told her it was carrot cake. Edith surprised me with a homemade carrot cake with fresh pineapple and lamb dinner the best I had ever had. I was really touched by her kindness.

After buying and reading "Turning Your Storms into Rainbows", I bought several more books to give away as gifts. The book is so moving I have read it three times. I am looking forward to reading her next book, "Turning Your Scars into Stars".

Elvira Gomes
91 years young
4 children
10 grandchildren
20 great grandchildren

What gift of wisdom did you receive from this testimony? ☆

How did this person turn their scars into stars? ☆

Testimony 18

About five years ago, Edie and I were walking on the beach and Edie happened to mention that she would be so excited when I had grandchildren because at this time I had no grandchildren and I have a son and daughter. I told Edie that my daughter was pretty sure she didn't want children and at that moment Edie stopped and immediately offered up a prayer, claiming the promises of blessings for my family in the form of grandchildren. Sure enough, within a year I had my first grandson, Nathan, and two years later a second grandson from my daughter named Nicholas. Later I asked Edie to pray for my son to have children. She hesitated and replied, "Well, I've never met him." Later he and his wife were visiting from Oregon and Edie met them at that time and started to pray very strong. Soon after my son called and announced that we were going to be grandparents of our first granddaughter, Kennedy. A couple years later we got another call from my son and are now grandparents of a new baby boy, Everett. My faith has been strengthened seeing God work through Edie for the good of the next generation. My testimony is that prayer works and my hope is that you'll be inspired to pray with someone and believe together for God's will.

Mary Bishop

Made in the USA
Columbia, SC
07 October 2024

43907906R00121